Fish and Sh

Jane Suthering

First published in 1998 for
Tesco Stores Limited
by Brilliant Books Ltd
84-86 Regent Street
London W1R 6DD

Origination by Colourpath Ltd, London
Printed and bound by Jarrold Book Printing,
Thetford, England

Fish and Shellfish

Jane Suthering

TESCO

About the author

Jane Suthering is the consultant food editor of the *Tesco Recipe Magazine* and author of many cookbooks. Her passion for fish began at the age of four, when she had her first prawn cocktail, in Whitby, on England's north-east coast. Jane still goes back there – for 'some of the best fish and chips in the country'.

Photographer	Jean Cazals
Home economist	Marie-Ange Lapierre
Stylist	Antonia Gaunt
Recipes tested by	Terry Farris
	Jan Fullwood
	Becky Johnson

CONTENTS

INTRODUCTION

The recipes in this book have been created and photographed specially for Tesco. They have been thoroughly tested and all the ingredients are normally available at larger Tesco stores, when in season. There is no need for any special kitchen equipment.

Using the recipes

1 Both metric and imperial weights and measures are given, except for goods sold in standard size packaging, such as cans. As conversions cannot always be exact, you should follow either the metric or the imperial throughout the recipe where possible.

2 British standard level spoon measurements are used. A tablespoon measure is equivalent to 15ml; a teaspoon measure is equivalent to 5ml.

3 Dishes cooked in the oven should be placed in the centre, unless otherwise stated. Tesco advises that all fish and eggs should be cooked thoroughly.

4 Some of the recipes include nuts or nut derivatives. These should not be eaten by children, people who have an allergic reaction to nuts, or women who are either pregnant or breastfeeding. It is advisable to check the labelling of any commercially prepared products to ensure that they do not contain nuts or nut derivatives.

5 Recipes containing sesame seeds or sesame products should not be eaten by children, the elderly, or women who are either pregnant or breastfeeding.

6 Vegetables and fruits are medium-sized, unless otherwise stated. If cooking or serving vegetables or fruits with their skins on, make sure that they are thoroughly rinsed.

7 The fat and calorie content of each recipe is given. These figures are for one serving only.

8 Each recipe has a simplicity rating of 1, 2 or 3 chef hats. Recipes with 1 hat are easy; those with 2 or 3 will require a little more effort.

SMOKED TROUT RILLETTES

Serves 4
Preparation 15 mins plus 30 mins chilling
Calories 163
Fat 11g
Simplicity

1 Flake the fish into a bowl and combine with the lemon rind and juice, sherry, softened butter and capers. Alternatively, blend the ingredients in a food processor or use a hand blender.

2 Spoon the mixture into small bowls or ramekins. Pour over the melted butter, if using, and garnish with the herbs or capers, if using. Cover and place in the fridge for 30 minutes or until the butter has set.

- 2 x 120g packs smoked trout fillets
- Finely grated rind and juice of 1 lemon
- 2 tbsp dry sherry
- 40g (1½oz) butter, softened, plus 40g (1½oz) butter, melted, for sealing (optional)
- 1 tsp capers, drained and chopped, plus extra to garnish (optional)
- Fresh herbs to garnish (optional)

A smooth smoky starter that's made in an instant. It will keep in the fridge for up to two days. Serve with crunchy Melba toast or on little cheese biscuits at a drinks party.

ITALIAN TUNA AND BEAN SALAD

Simplicity

Serves 4
Preparation 15 mins

Calories 339
Fat 25g

- 198g can tuna in oil, drained and oil reserved
- 400g can borlotti beans, drained and rinsed
- 1 small red onion, thinly sliced
- 2 sticks celery, thinly sliced
- 3 tbsp chopped fresh flat-leaf parsley

For the dressing

- 4 tbsp olive oil
- 2 tbsp balsamic or white wine vinegar
- Salt and black pepper

1 To make the dressing, whisk the reserved tuna oil with the olive oil and vinegar, then season.

2 Flake the tuna into a large bowl and mix with the borlotti beans, red onion, celery and parsley. Spoon over the dressing and toss well to combine.

The combination of colours, flavours and textures in this simple salad has made it a real favourite in Italy. It's delicious served with some warmed ciabatta bread.

SMOKED MACKEREL, ORANGE AND LENTIL SALAD

Serves 4
Preparation 15 mins
Cooking 30 mins

Calories 506
Fat 39g

Simplicity 

1 Cook the lentils in a saucepan of boiling water for 30 minutes or until tender.

2 Meanwhile, slice the top and bottom off each orange, using a small serrated knife – work over a bowl to catch the juices. Cut away the peel and pith, following the curve of the fruit, then carefully cut between the membranes to release the segments. Squeeze the juice from the membranes into the bowl and reserve for the dressing. Arrange the watercress, orange segments and smoked mackerel in serving bowls.

3 To make the dressing, mix together the horseradish, oil, seasoning and the reserved orange juice. Drain the lentils, stir into the dressing, then spoon over the salad and serve.

50g (2oz) lentilles vertes
4 small oranges
2 x 85g packs watercress
400g (14oz) smoked mackerel fillet, skinned and coarsely flaked

For the dressing
4 tbsp horseradish cream
4 tbsp vegetable oil
Salt and black pepper

The combination of smoked fish, small green lentils and horseradish is fabulous. The peppery watercress and sweet orange segments complete the taste sensation.

SMOKED SALMON SUMMER PLATTER

Simplicity

Serves 4
Preparation 10 mins
Cooking 15 mins

Calories 229
Fat 13g

- 275g (10oz) small new potatoes
- Salt and black pepper
- 24 thin asparagus spears
- 1 tbsp chopped fresh dill, plus extra to garnish
- 100ml (4fl oz) crème fraîche
- 175g (6oz) smoked salmon, thinly sliced

1 Cook the potatoes in boiling salted water for 15 minutes or until tender, then drain well.

2 Meanwhile, cut the coarse ends off the asparagus spears. Cook the asparagus in boiling salted water for 3-4 minutes, until just tender. Drain well.

3 Stir the chopped dill into the crème fraîche, then season to taste. Arrange the asparagus and potatoes on plates, then top with the salmon slices. Grind over a little pepper and garnish with dill. Serve with the herby crème fraîche.

Serve this dish in May when English asparagus is at its best and Jersey potatoes are available. Other varieties of new or waxy potatoes will taste good too.

PRAWN AND AVOCADO COCKTAIL

Serves 4
Preparation 15 mins

Calories 574
Fat 50g

Simplicity 🍳

- 400g (14oz) cooked peeled prawns, defrosted if frozen
- 8 tbsp mayonnaise
- 4 tbsp tomato ketchup
- 2 sticks celery, finely chopped
- 1 spring onion, finely sliced, or 1 tbsp finely chopped onion
- Salt and black pepper
- 2 avocados
- Squeeze of lemon juice

1 Mix together the prawns, mayonnaise and tomato ketchup in a bowl, then stir in the celery and onion and season to taste.

2 Halve the avocados, remove the stones and peel. Dice the flesh, then toss in the lemon juice to stop it browning. Add to the prawn mixture, stirring lightly, then transfer to glasses or serving plates and grind over a little pepper.

A classic starter that's even better when you add chunks of ripe avocado. This gives four generous portions, so you could also serve it with crisp leaves as a salad.

FRESH CRAB WITH A MUSTARD-DRESSED SALAD

Simplicity

Serves 4
Preparation 15 mins

Calories 253
Fat 21g

- 4 Little Gem lettuces, shredded
- 3 tbsp snipped fresh chives
- 2 dressed crabs

For the dressing

- 2 tbsp Dijon mustard
- 2 tbsp white wine vinegar
- 6 tbsp vegetable oil
- Pinch of sugar
- Salt and black pepper

1 To make the dressing, mix together the mustard, vinegar, oil, sugar and seasoning.

2 Place the lettuce and 2 tablespoons of the chives in a bowl, pour over the dressing and toss well. Arrange in bowls, top with the crabmeat and garnish with the remaining chives.

Fresh crab is so good that you don't need to do anything too elaborate with it. Buttered brown bread and this simple salad in a light mustardy dressing are all you need.

SARDINES STUFFED WITH SPINACH AND PINE NUTS

Serves 4
Preparation 25 mins
Cooking 15 mins

Calories 284
Fat 18g

Simplicity 

- 8 fresh sardines
- Salt and black pepper
- 2 tbsp olive oil
- 1 shallot, finely chopped
- 1 tbsp pine nut kernels
- 175g (6oz) frozen leaf spinach, defrosted and excess moisture squeezed out
- 1 tbsp sultanas
- 2 tbsp fresh breadcrumbs
- 1 tbsp lime juice

1 Preheat the oven to 220°C/425°F/Gas Mark 7. Remove the scales from the fish by scraping from the tail end with the back of a small knife. Cut off the heads, then slice along the belly and remove the guts. Open out each fish and place skin-side up on the work surface. Press along the length of the backbone with your thumb, then turn the fish over and ease out the backbone, cutting it at the tail end but leaving the tail intact. Rinse and pat dry with kitchen towels, season and turn in 1 tablespoon of the oil.

2 Heat the remaining oil in a frying pan and fry the shallot and pine nut kernels for 2-3 minutes, until golden. Remove from the heat, then stir in the spinach, sultanas, 1 tablespoon of the breadcrumbs and the lime juice. Season, then use the mixture to sandwich the sardines together in pairs, skin-side out.

3 Lay the sardines on a baking sheet, sprinkle with the remaining breadcrumbs and bake for 10 minutes or until golden and cooked through.

Fresh sardines are easy to fillet and this fruit, nut and spinach filling will change your view of them for ever!

RED MULLET SALTIMBOCCA

Simplicity

Serves 4
Preparation 30 mins plus 30 mins chilling

Cooking 6 mins
Calories 371
Fat 20g

- 4 red mullet, about 250g (9oz) each, filleted
- Salt and black pepper
- 16 fresh sage leaves
- 4 thin slices prosciutto crudo, such as Parma ham, halved lengthways
- 25g (1oz) butter
- 2 tbsp olive oil
- Lemon wedges to serve

1 Wipe the fish fillets, then remove any scales by scraping from the tail end with the back of a knife. Remove any fine bones with a pair of tweezers.

2 Season lightly, then press 2 sage leaves onto one side of each fillet and wrap in a slice of prosciutto. Cover and leave in the fridge for 30 minutes, or up to 8 hours to allow the flavours to mingle.

3 Heat the butter and oil in a large frying pan. Place the fish in the pan, sage-side down, and cook for 2-3 minutes, until crisp. Turn over and cook for a further 2-3 minutes, until the fish is opaque and the outside crisp and deep red. Serve with lemon wedges.

Red mullet tastes great in this crispy prosciutto wrapping, which helps to stop the fish drying out as it cooks. But make sure you remove all the small bones from the fish.

SPICY DEEP-FRIED SQUID RINGS

Serves 4
Preparation 10 mins
Cooking 8 mins

Calories 304
Fat 14g

Simplicity

- 6 tbsp plain flour
- 2 tbsp paprika
- 1 tsp salt
- 450g (1lb) fresh squid, cut into rings, or frozen squid rings, defrosted and dried
- Vegetable oil for deep-frying

1 Mix together the flour, paprika and salt. Toss the squid rings in the seasoned flour to coat evenly.

2 Heat 5cm (2in) of vegetable oil in a large heavy-based saucepan. Test that the oil is ready by adding a squid ring – it should sizzle at once. Cook a quarter of the rings for 1-2 minutes, until golden. Drain on kitchen towels and keep warm while you cook the remaining rings in 3 more batches.

Deep-fried squid rings are always good when they're freshly made – these have a little extra spice. Serve them as a starter or a pre-dinner nibble with some mayonnaise.

THAI FISH STICKS WITH CUCUMBER SALAD

Simplicity 2

Serves 4
Preparation 25 mins
Cooking 6 mins

Calories 183
Fat 3g

- 4 spring onions, chopped
- Small handful of fresh coriander
- 450g (1lb) cod loin or other skinless white fish fillet, cubed
- 3 tbsp red curry paste
- 1 tsp salt
- 2 tsp lime juice
- 1 large egg white
- 12 stalks lemon grass

For the salad

- ½ cucumber, peeled and very thinly sliced
- 4 tbsp white wine vinegar
- 4 tbsp white sugar
- 1 large red or green chilli, deseeded and finely chopped
- 1 small shallot, thinly sliced

1 To make the salad, combine the cucumber, vinegar, sugar, chilli and shallot with 4 tablespoons of cold water. Cover and leave in a cool place until needed.

2 To make the fish sticks, blend the spring onions and coriander in a food processor until finely chopped, or use a hand blender. Add the fish, curry paste, salt and lime juice and blend until the fish is finely chopped. Add the egg white and continue blending until the mixture is stiff.

3 Divide the fish mixture into 12 portions, then carefully press each around a lemon grass stick, forming a 'sausage' shape. Preheat the grill to high. Place the fish sticks on a lightly oiled baking sheet, then grill for 6 minutes, turning once, until cooked and lightly browned on all sides. Serve with the cucumber salad.

Cooking these spicy kebabs on lemon grass sticks gives them a lovely citrus flavour. The simple salad combines slivers of cool cucumber with a little red-hot chilli.

GRILLED OYSTERS WITH CHAMPAGNE AND CREAM

Serves 4
Preparation 40 mins
Cooking 5 mins

Calories 114
Fat 9g

Simplicity  

1 To open each oyster, place a thick cloth on a work surface and put the shell on top, flat side up. Wrap a cloth round your hand and insert a small sharp knife between the halves opposite the hinge. Taking care not to cut yourself, work the knife back and forth to loosen the muscle attached to the inside of the flat shell, then prise open. Scoop out each oyster with a teaspoon and strain the juices into a small saucepan. Remove and discard the muscle from the 12 rounded half-shells, then wash and dry. Place in a flameproof dish lined with crumpled foil so that they sit level.

2 Bring the juices to a simmer and poach the oysters for 30-60 seconds, until just firm. Remove from the pan. Add the champagne to the pan and boil for 2 minutes to reduce. Remove from the heat and whisk in the butter, then the cream. Season with pepper.

3 Preheat the grill to high. Cook the spinach in a saucepan for 2-3 minutes, until wilted. Squeeze out the excess liquid and divide between the shells. Top with an oyster and spoon over a little sauce. Cook close to the grill for 1 minute or until heated through.

- 12 fresh oysters
- 3 tbsp champagne, dry sparkling wine or dry vermouth
- 25g (1oz) butter
- 2 tbsp double cream
- Black pepper
- 125g (4oz) baby spinach

This is the perfect dish for anyone who loves the taste of oysters but not their texture when they're uncooked.

SMOKED HADDOCK WITH CHIVE BUTTER SAUCE

Simplicity 

Serves 4
Preparation 15 mins
Cooking 15 mins

Calories 446
Fat 33g

- 4 pieces smoked haddock fillet with skin, about 175g (6oz) each
- 250g bag fresh spinach, stalks removed
- Salt and black pepper

For the sauce

- 3 shallots, finely chopped
- 6 tbsp dry white wine
- 6 tbsp white wine vinegar
- 150g (5oz) unsalted butter, diced
- 3 tbsp snipped fresh chives

1 To make the sauce, place the shallots, wine and 5 tablespoons of the vinegar in a saucepan. Boil for 5-10 minutes, until the liquid has reduced to 1 tablespoon. Strain, discard the shallots, then return the reduced liquid to the pan and set aside.

2 Place the fish, side-by-side and skin-side down, in a large saucepan. Just cover with cold water and pour over the remaining vinegar. Slowly bring to a simmer, then cover and remove from the heat and set aside.

3 Place the spinach in a large pan and cook for 3-4 minutes, until wilted. Squeeze out any excess liquid, then season. Heat through the reserved wine liquid, then whisk in the butter to give a creamy sauce. Add the chives and season. Drain the fish thoroughly, arrange on plates with the spinach, then drizzle over the chive butter sauce.

Wilted spinach and a chive butter sauce complement the haddock's smoky flavour perfectly. You can use dyed or undyed fish for this dish. Serve with some new potatoes.

SWORDFISH WITH LIME AND CORIANDER BUTTER

Serves 4
Preparation 15 mins plus 15 mins marinating
Cooking 8 mins
Calories 309
Fat 20g
Simplicity 

1 Mix together the oil, lime juice and seasoning in a shallow non-metallic bowl. Add the fish steaks and turn to coat. Cover and marinate in the fridge for at least 15 minutes or up to 8 hours.

2 To make the lime and coriander butter, beat the butter until smooth, then slowly beat in the lime rind and juice and the coriander. Season, then shape into a small roll, wrap in baking paper and refrigerate.

3 Preheat the grill to high. Cook the swordfish close to the heat source for 4 minutes on each side, until lightly browned and cooked through. Unwrap the butter and cut into slices, discarding the paper. Serve the fish topped with a slice of butter and garnished with coriander.

- 1 tbsp vegetable oil
- Juice of 1 lime
- Salt and black pepper
- 4 swordfish steaks, about 175g (6oz) each

For the butter

- 50g (2oz) butter, softened
- Finely grated rind and juice of 1 lime
- 2 tbsp chopped fresh coriander, plus extra to garnish

Cooking swordfish quickly under the grill or in the frying pan helps to keep it really moist and succulent. Serve with rice or couscous flavoured with peppers and spring onion.

GRILLED SALMON STEAKS WITH MINT VINAIGRETTE

Simplicity

Serves 4
Preparation 10 mins
Cooking 10 mins

Calories 470
Fat 38g

- 4 salmon steaks, about 175g (6oz) each
- Salt and black pepper

For the vinaigrette

- 2 tbsp chopped fresh mint, plus extra leaves to garnish
- 1 small shallot, finely chopped
- 6 tbsp olive or vegetable oil
- Juice of 1 lemon

1 Preheat the grill to high and line the grill tray with kitchen foil. Place the salmon steaks on top and season lightly. Grill for 4-5 minutes on each side, until lightly browned and cooked through.

2 Meanwhile, make the vinaigrette. Mix together the mint, shallot, oil and lemon juice, then season to taste. Spoon over the salmon steaks and garnish with mint.

This minty vinaigrette is very easy to make but it gives a new twist to salmon. You can also use the vinaigrette to dress a cucumber and potato salad to serve with it.

MACKEREL KEBABS WITH GOOSEBERRY SAUCE

Serves 4
Preparation 10 mins plus 10 mins soaking
Cooking 25 mins
Calories 641
Fat 47g
Simplicity

1 To make the sauce, heat the butter and oil in a saucepan and gently fry the onion and fennel, covered, for 10 minutes or until softened. Add the gooseberries and sugar and cook for 10 minutes or until the vegetables and gooseberries are tender. Season to taste.

2 Meanwhile, soak 8 wooden skewers in cold water for at least 10 minutes. Preheat the grill to high, then thread the mackerel onto the skewers. Brush the fish with oil and season.

3 Grill the kebabs for 5 minutes, turning occasionally, until the fish flesh is opaque and the skin lightly charred. Serve with the sauce.

- 4 mackerel, about 375g (13oz) each, filleted and cut into bite-sized pieces
- Olive oil for brushing

For the sauce

- 25g (1oz) butter
- 1 tbsp vegetable oil
- 1 onion, thinly sliced
- 1 bulb fennel, thinly sliced
- 175g (6oz) gooseberries
- 25g (1oz) sugar
- Salt and black pepper

Sharp fruit sauces, such as gooseberry and rhubarb, are natural partners for the richness of these grilled mackerel kebabs. The fennel adds a subtle aniseed flavour.

FRIED FILLETS OF PLAICE WITH ANCHOVY BUTTER

Simplicity

Serves 4
Preparation 10 mins
Cooking 6 mins

Calories 380
Fat 22g

- 4 large plaice fillets
- 2 tbsp plain flour
- 2 tbsp vegetable oil or oil from the drained anchovies
- Fresh chives to garnish

For the butter

- 50g can anchovy fillets in olive oil, drained
- 50g (2oz) unsalted butter, softened
- 1 tbsp lemon juice
- Salt and black pepper

1 To make the anchovy butter, blend the anchovies, butter, lemon juice and plenty of pepper until smooth in a food processor, or with a hand blender. Alternatively, mash the anchovies and beat in the other ingredients with a spoon. Shape into a small roll, wrap in baking paper, then place in the refrigerator.

2 Season the plaice fillets and dust with the flour. Heat 1 tablespoon of oil in a large heavy-based frying pan over a high heat, add 2 plaice fillets, skin-side up, and fry for 1 minute or until golden brown. Turn over and fry for 2 minutes or until browned. Remove from the pan and keep warm. Wipe the pan and cook the remaining fillets in the same way. Unwrap the butter roll and cut into slices, discarding the paper. Serve the fish with a slice of anchovy butter on top, garnished with chives.

The natural saltiness of anchovies goes beautifully with the delicate flavour of the fried plaice. Serve with some green beans for their fresh flavour and colour.

TUNA NICOISE

Serves 4
Preparation 10 mins
Cooking 15 mins

Calories 378
Fat 21g

Simplicity

1 Cook the beans in boiling salted water for 3-5 minutes, until tender but still firm to the bite. Drain, refresh under cold water and set aside. Place 2 tablespoons of the oil in a shallow bowl, add the tuna and turn to coat, then season lightly.

2 Heat a large heavy-based frying pan over a high heat, then add the tuna and cook for 1 minute on each side. Reduce the heat and cook for a further 1-2 minutes on each side, until the steaks have slightly browned. Set aside.

3 Heat the remaining oil in the pan and fry the red pepper for 1 minute or until softened. Add the beans, tomatoes and olives and stir-fry for 1 minute to warm through. Remove from the heat and pour in the vinegar. Serve the tuna topped with the pepper mixture and scatter over the parsley or coriander.

- 170g pack fine green beans, cut in 7.5cm (3in) lengths
- 4 tbsp olive oil
- 4 tuna steaks, about 175g (6oz) each and 2.5cm (1in) thick
- Salt and black pepper
- 1 red pepper, deseeded and diced
- 12 cherry tomatoes, halved
- 16 pitted black olives
- 1 tbsp balsamic vinegar
- Fresh flat-leaf parsley or coriander to garnish

If you've never tried fresh tuna, give it a go in this traditional and refreshing combination. It's a wonderful main course, especially with some sliced new potatoes.

NUT-CRUSTED HUSS BITES

Simplicity

Serves 4
Preparation 15 mins
Cooking 15 mins

Calories 417
Fat 30g

- 50g (2oz) chopped hazelnuts
- 50g (2oz) fresh breadcrumbs
- 25g (1oz) plain flour
- Salt and black pepper
- 1 large egg, beaten
- 500g (1lb 2oz) huss fillet, cut into 20 even-sized pieces
- Vegetable oil for shallow frying
- Tartare sauce, vinegar or lemon juice to serve

1 Mix together the nuts and breadcrumbs in a large shallow bowl. Put the flour into another bowl and season. Put the egg into a third bowl. Dip the fish pieces into the flour, then into the egg and finally into the breadcrumb mixture to coat.

2 Heat 1cm (½in) of oil in a large frying pan and fry a third of the fish pieces for 5 minutes or until golden on all sides. Drain on kitchen towels and keep warm while you cook the rest in 2 batches. Serve with tartare sauce or sprinkled with vinegar or lemon juice.

Hazelnuts go particularly well with fish and make a delightful crunchy coating for these tasty bite-sized pieces of tender huss. Serve them hot with a green salad.

FRIED SKATE WITH BLACK BUTTER

Serves 2
Preparation 5 mins
Cooking 15 mins

Calories 425
Fat 27g

Simplicity 2

1 Season the fish and dust with the flour. Heat the oil and 15g (½oz) of the butter in a large non-stick frying pan over a medium-high heat. Fry the skate for 5 minutes on each side or until crisp and golden and cooked through at the thickest part. Set aside and keep warm.

2 Heat the remaining butter in the pan until it turns nut brown. Add the vinegar, taking care as the mixture may spit, and bring almost to the boil, then stir in the capers and parsley. Heat through, then pour over the fish.

- Salt and black pepper
- 2 skate wings, about 225g (8oz) each
- 1 tbsp plain flour
- 1 tbsp vegetable oil
- 40g (1½oz) butter
- 2 tbsp white wine vinegar
- 2 tbsp capers, drained
- 2 tbsp chopped fresh parsley

Traditionally, skate is poached for this dish, but frying it gives a crisp golden crust. Serve with boiled potatoes, lemon wedges and your favourite green vegetable.

JAMAICAN TALAPIA

Simplicity 

Serves 4
Preparation 20 mins
Cooking 7 mins

Calories 392
Fat 20g

- 1 onion, chopped
- 2 cloves garlic, chopped
- 1 tsp each of dried marjoram and thyme
- ½ tsp dried crushed chillies
- ½ tsp Angostura bitters
- Salt and black pepper
- 4 talapia, about 300g (11oz) each, or 2 groupers, about 550g (1lb 4oz) each, filleted and skinned
- 1 large egg, beaten
- 3 tbsp plain flour
- Vegetable oil for shallow-frying

1 Blend the onion, garlic, herbs, chillies, bitters and ¼ teaspoon of salt to a paste in a food processor, or with a hand blender or pestle and mortar. Spread the paste over one side of each fillet.

2 Pour the beaten egg onto a large plate and spread the flour on another. Place a fillet, paste-side up, in the egg and spoon a little over the top. Transfer to the flour, still paste-side up, and dust the top with flour. Repeat with the remaining fillets.

3 Heat 5mm (¼in) of oil in a large non-stick frying pan over a high heat. Add the fillets, paste-side down, then cook for 3-4 minutes. Turn over and cook for a further 2-3 minutes, until golden brown and cooked through. Drain on kitchen towels.

These fish get the Caribbean treatment with a crisp, spicy coating which includes crushed chillies. Serve with chips or rice and a tomato, red onion and avocado salad.

CRISPY TROUT WITH ALMONDS AND GINGER JUICE

Serves 4
Preparation 10 mins
Cooking 12 mins
Calories 705
Fat 31g
Simplicity 1

1 Season the fish and dust with the flour. Heat the oil in a large non-stick frying pan over a medium-high heat, add the fish and cook for 5 minutes on each side or until crisp, golden and cooked through. Remove from the pan and keep warm.

2 Meanwhile, squeeze the grated ginger over a small bowl to extract the juice – you should have 4-6 teaspoons.

3 Add the butter and almonds to the frying pan and cook gently for 2 minutes or until the nuts are golden. Add the currants and ginger juice, heat through for a few seconds, then spoon over the fish.

- Salt and black pepper
- 4 rainbow trout, cleaned and boned, heads removed if liked
- 2 tbsp plain flour
- 2 tbsp vegetable oil
- 75g (3oz) fresh root ginger, grated
- 25g (1oz) butter
- 75g (3oz) flaked almonds
- 2 tbsp currants

Dusting the fish with flour before you fry it makes the skin really crispy. And if you don't like eating the skin, it will peel off in one go to reveal the lovely pink flesh.

FISH AND CHIPS WITH TARTARE SAUCE

Simplicity 2

Serves 4
Preparation 30 mins
Cooking 35 mins

Calories 1088
Fat 71g

- 75g (3oz) plain flour
- ¼ tsp salt
- 1 tbsp vegetable oil
- 4 large potatoes, cut into chunky chips
- Oil for deep-frying
- 1 large egg white
- 4 pieces cod loin, about 175g (6oz) each
- Salt flakes to serve

For the tartare sauce

- 150ml (¼ pint) mayonnaise
- 1 tbsp capers, drained and chopped
- 1 tbsp chopped gherkin
- 1 tbsp chopped fresh parsley
- 1 tsp finely chopped shallot or spring onion

1 To make the sauce, combine the mayonnaise, capers, gherkin, parsley and shallot or spring onion in a bowl. Cover and place in the fridge. Mix the flour, salt and oil with 100ml (4fl oz) of cold water to make a batter.

2 Cover the chips with cold water, then drain and dry on kitchen towels. Heat the oil in a large heavy-based saucepan. Test that the oil is ready by adding a potato chip – it should sizzle immediately. Cook the chips in 3 or 4 batches for 5-7 minutes each, until golden and cooked. Drain on kitchen towels and keep warm. Whisk the egg white until stiff (this is easiest with an electric whisk) and fold into the batter.

3 Reduce the heat a little and drop a teaspoon of batter into the oil – it should bubble and firm up straight away. Dip the pieces of fish into the batter, coating well, then cook for 5-7 minutes, until crisp and golden, then drain on kitchen towels. Serve sprinkled with salt, with the chips and tartare sauce.

There's nothing ordinary about fish and chips when the batter is crunchy and the chips are golden and crisp. This luxurious tartare sauce adds the finishing touch.

DOVER SOLE WITH LEMON AND PARSLEY BUTTER

Serves 4
Preparation 15 mins
Cooking 15 mins

Calories 283
Fat 19g

Simplicity 

1 Preheat the oven to 200°C/400°F/Gas Mark 6. Butter a large baking sheet.

2 Cut away the 'frill' of fins along each side of the fish with a pair of scissors. With a sharp knife, score a line about 1cm (½in) in from the sides of the fish, on both sides.

3 Melt the butter in a small saucepan. Place the fish, dark-side up, on the baking sheet, brush with melted butter, then sprinkle with the salt flakes and pepper. Reserve the remaining melted butter. Cook the fish for 15 minutes or until the flesh is white and cooked through.

4 Add the lemon juice, parsley and any cooking juices to the reserved butter and heat through, stirring. Spoon over the sole.

- 75g (3oz) butter, plus extra for greasing
- 4 Dover sole, about 350g (12oz) each, scaled, gutted and cleaned
- 2 tsp salt flakes
- Black pepper
- Juice of 1 lemon
- 2 tbsp chopped fresh parsley

Dover sole should be treated simply – butter, parsley, lemon juice and seasoning are all it needs. Scoring the fish before cooking makes it easier to remove the skin.

TANDOORI COLEY FILLETS WITH CUCUMBER RAITA

Simplicity

Serves 4
Preparation 15 mins
plus 2 hrs marinating

Cooking 20 mins
Calories 312
Fat 10g

- 2 tbsp hot curry powder
- 2 tsp garam masala
- 2 tbsp vegetable oil
- 2 tbsp lime juice
- 1-2 cloves garlic, crushed
- 1-2 chillies, deseeded and finely chopped (optional)
- ½ tsp salt
- 2 coley fillets, about 450g (1lb) each, skinned and each cut into 4 pieces

For the raita

- 2 tsp cumin seeds
- 1 cucumber, peeled, deseeded and thinly sliced or chopped
- 2 x 150g cartons natural yogurt
- Salt and black pepper

1 Mix together the curry powder, garam masala, oil, lime juice, garlic, chillies, if using, and salt in a large non-metallic bowl. Add the fish and turn to coat. Cover and leave in the fridge for 2 hours, or overnight.

2 Preheat the oven to 220°C/425°F/Gas Mark 7. Place the fish in an ovenproof dish and cook for 15-20 minutes, until firm and cooked through.

3 Meanwhile, make the cucumber raita. Put the cumin seeds into a small frying pan and fry gently for 2 minutes to release their flavour. Mix with the cucumber and yogurt in a small bowl, then season to taste. Serve with the fish.

A pungent mix of spices turns this inexpensive white fish into an exotic golden treat. Serve with some warmed naan bread and a tomato and onion salad.

COD FILLET WITH CHEDDAR AND TOMATO TOPPING

Serves 4
Preparation 15 mins
Cooking 25 mins

Calories 391
Fat 24g

Simplicity 

- Butter for greasing
- 150g (5oz) mature Cheddar, grated
- 4 tsp wholegrain mustard
- 4 tbsp crème fraîche
- 4 pieces thick cod loin, each about 175g (6oz)
- Salt and black pepper
- 3 tomatoes, sliced

1 Preheat the oven to 200°C/400°F/Gas Mark 6 and grease 4 individual gratin dishes.

2 Mix together the Cheddar, mustard and crème fraîche. Place a piece of fish in each dish and season lightly. Top with the tomato slices, then spoon over the cheese mixture.

3 Cook at the top of the oven for 25 minutes, until the cheese has melted and is turning golden and the fish is firm and cooked through.

Mature Cheddar, mustard and crème fraîche give this simple dish a slight tang. Choose thick cod loin for this recipe or, if you can't get it, buy fillets and fold them in half.

LEMON-SCENTED FISH PIE

Simplicity 

Serves 4
Preparation 20 mins
Cooking 1 hr

Calories 464
Fat 13g

- 1kg (2lb 4oz) potatoes, cut into even-sized pieces
- Salt and black pepper
- 50g (2oz) butter
- 1 onion, chopped
- 2 sticks celery, sliced
- 2 tbsp plain flour
- 250ml (9fl oz) fish stock
- Finely grated rind and juice of 1 large lemon
- 450g (1lb) cod loin, cut into cubes
- 175g (6oz) cooked and shelled mussels
- 2 tbsp chopped fresh parsley
- 4 tbsp milk

1 Cook the potatoes in boiling salted water for 15-20 minutes, until tender, then drain.

2 Meanwhile, melt 25g (1oz) of the butter in a large saucepan, then add the onion and celery and cook for 2-3 minutes, until softened. Add the flour and cook, stirring, for 1 minute, then slowly add the fish stock and cook, stirring, until thickened. Add the lemon rind and juice and season with pepper.

3 Preheat the oven to 220°C/425°F/Gas Mark 7. Remove the sauce from the heat, stir in the cod, mussels and parsley, then transfer to an ovenproof dish. Mash the potatoes with the remaining butter and the milk. Season, then spread evenly over the fish with a fork. Cook in the oven for 30-40 minutes, until the sauce is bubbling and the topping is starting to brown.

Creamy mashed potatoes make a wonderful topping for this lemon-flavoured cod and mussel pie. If you want to, replace the mussels with peeled prawns.

KIPPER KEDGEREE

Serves 4
Preparation 20 mins
plus 5 mins standing

Cooking 20 mins
Calories 756
Fat 39g

Simplicity 🍴

- 250g (9oz) basmati rice
- 4 large eggs
- 4 smoked kipper fillets
- 75g (3oz) butter
- 1 onion, finely chopped
- 8 tbsp chopped fresh parsley
- 3 tbsp lemon juice
- Salt and black pepper

1 Rinse the rice thoroughly, then cook according to the packet instructions. Drain and leave to cool. Put the eggs into a saucepan of cold water. Bring to the boil and cook for 10 minutes. Peel under cold running water, then shell and roughly chop.

2 Meanwhile, place the kippers in a dish and cover with boiling water. Leave to stand for 5 minutes. Drain, remove the skin, roughly flake the fish and discard any visible bones.

3 Melt half the butter in a large non-stick frying pan, then add the onion and cook for 4 minutes or until softened. Add the rice and mix well, then add the eggs, kippers, parsley, lemon juice, seasoning and the remaining butter, and heat through thoroughly.

If you like the strong smoky flavour of kippers, you'll love this kedgeree. It's traditionally served for breakfast, but it also makes a great lunch or supper dish with salad.

CHINESE-STYLE STEAMED GREY MULLET

Simplicity 

Serves 2

Preparation 10 mins plus 30 mins marinating

Cooking 20 mins

Calories 345

Fat 15g

- 1 grey mullet, about 700g (1lb 9oz), scaled, gutted and cleaned
- ½ tsp salt
- 1 tbsp vegetable oil
- 1 tbsp light soy sauce
- 1 large carrot, cut into fine strips
- 4 spring onions, cut into fine strips
- 1 tbsp grated fresh root ginger
- 1 tbsp sesame oil (optional)
- Fresh coriander to garnish

1 Make 4 deep slashes along each side of the fish, then rub the fish inside and out with the salt, vegetable oil and soy sauce. Cover and place in the fridge for 30 minutes.

2 Spread half the carrot, spring onions and ginger on a large piece of foil. Place the fish on top, then sprinkle with the remaining vegetables and ginger and any remaining marinade. Loosely fold over the foil to seal. Transfer the fish to a steamer. Alternatively, transfer to a plate, then place on a rack set over a roasting tin half filled with water. Cover tightly with a lid or with foil.

3 Cook for 20 minutes or until the fish is firm and cooked through. Put the sesame oil, if using, into a small saucepan and heat. Drizzle over the fish and garnish with coriander.

The strong flavours of ginger, spring onion, sesame and soy work really well with grey mullet, which has a lovely soft texture and is a much underrated fish.

MONKFISH BOURGUIGNON

Serves 4
Preparation 20 mins
Cooking 50 mins
Calories 547
Fat 34g
Simplicity 2

1 To make the sauce, heat 1 tablespoon of the oil and 15g (½oz) of the butter in a pan. Cook the onion, 50g (2oz) of the bacon and the chopped mushrooms for 5 minutes or until the onion is golden. Stir in the flour and cook for 1 minute. Stir in the wine and stock. Add the herbs and pepper. Simmer, covered, for 30 minutes, stirring occasionally.

2 Meanwhile, put the pickling onions into boiling water for 2 minutes, then drain, dry and skin them. Heat the remaining oil and 15g (½oz) of the butter in a frying pan and fry the onions for 5 minutes. Add the remaining bacon and cook for 5 minutes or until crisp. Remove from the pan. Cook the fish in 2 batches for 1 minute, turning to brown on all sides, then remove from the pan. Melt the rest of the butter and cook the whole mushrooms for 2-3 minutes.

3 Strain the sauce into a clean pan and add the pickling onions and bacon. Cook gently for 10 minutes, then add the monkfish and mushrooms and cook for a further 5 minutes, until the fish is cooked through. Season and serve garnished with parsley.

- 2 tbsp vegetable oil
- 40g (1½oz) butter
- 1 onion, chopped
- 175g (6oz) rindless streaky bacon, chopped
- 175g (6oz) button mushrooms, 50g (2oz) chopped, the rest left whole
- 2 tbsp plain flour
- 450ml (¾ pint) red wine
- 300ml (½ pint) fish or chicken stock
- 1 dried bay leaf
- Fresh thyme sprigs
- Salt and black pepper
- 12 pickling onions
- 550g (1lb 4oz) monkfish fillet, cut into cubes
- Chopped fresh parsley to garnish

Some people think that red wine and fish don't go – but this fantastic dish proves just how wrong they are.

WHOLE ROAST SEA BASS WITH LEMON AND BASIL

Simplicity

Serves 4
Preparation 15 mins
Cooking 20 mins

Calories 433
Fat 28g

- 8 tbsp olive oil
- 4 sea bass, about 300g (11oz) each, scaled, gutted and cleaned
- 24 large basil leaves
- Pared rind of 1 large lemon and 2 tbsp juice
- 6 small tomatoes, halved
- 2 tsp salt flakes
- Black pepper

1 Preheat the oven to 220°C/425°F/Gas Mark 7. Put the olive oil into a large ovenproof dish, add the fish and turn to coat, then tuck 3 basil leaves and a little lemon rind into the belly of each fish. Place the tomatoes in the dish and sprinkle over the remaining basil and lemon rind. Season the fish and tomatoes.

2 Cook the fish in the oven for 20 minutes or until the flesh is firm and cooked through. Sprinkle with lemon juice.

Sea bass should not be swamped by strong flavours or a sauce that's too heavy or rich. Lemon and basil are the perfect partners for its delicate taste and texture.

TURBOT WITH ORANGE AND TARRAGON SAUCE

Serves 2
Preparation 20 mins
Cooking 30 mins

Calories 595
Fat 35g

Simplicity 

1 Preheat the oven to 200°C/400°F/Gas Mark 6. Put 5 tablespoons of water into an ovenproof dish the same size as the fish. Season the fish, then place in the dish and dot with butter. Cook for 30 minutes or until the flesh is firm and cooked through.

2 Meanwhile, make the sauce. Melt the butter in a saucepan and cook the shallot and orange rind for 5 minutes or until softened. Add the wine, stock and tarragon stalks and bring to the boil. Cook briskly for 10 minutes, then strain into a clean pan. Mix the citrus juices with the cornflour, then stir into the sauce and simmer for 2-3 minutes, until slightly thickened. Remove from the heat and stir in the cream or butter, chopped tarragon and seasoning.

3 Cut the fish from head to tail, along the backbone, cutting to the bone. Remove the skin, then lift off the 2 fillets with a knife. Remove the bone to reveal the remaining 2 fillets. Serve with the sauce.

- 1kg (2lb 4oz) whole turbot, gutted, cleaned and trimmed
- Salt and black pepper
- 25g (1oz) butter

For the sauce

- 25g (1oz) butter
- 1 shallot, finely chopped
- Pared rind and juice of ½ large orange
- 100ml (4fl oz) dry white wine
- 200ml (7fl oz) fish stock
- 1 tbsp chopped fresh tarragon, stalks reserved
- Juice of ½ lemon
- 2 tsp cornflour
- 2 tbsp double cream or 25g (1oz) butter

Turbot is expensive, but many people think it's the finest fish of all. The orange and tarragon sauce makes the most of its flavour. Serve with sugar snaps and carrot batons.

BELGIAN-STYLE MUSSELS

Simplicity 

Serves 4
Preparation 30 mins
Cooking 10 mins

Calories 324
Fat 25g

- 1.8kg (4lb) mussels in their shells
- 25g (1oz) butter
- 1 tbsp vegetable oil
- 4 shallots or 1 onion, chopped
- 2 sticks celery, chopped, plus any leaves
- 150ml (¼ pint) dry white wine
- Black pepper
- 142ml carton whipping or double cream
- 4 tbsp chopped fresh flat-leaf parsley

1 Scrub the mussels under cold running water, then pull away any beards and discard any mussels that are open or damaged. Heat the butter and oil in a very large saucepan, then add the shallots or onion and celery and cook for 2-3 minutes, until the shallots are translucent.

2 Stir in the wine and plenty of pepper and bring to the boil. Add the mussels, cover and cook over a high heat, shaking the pan occasionally, for 4-5 minutes, until the mussels have opened. Remove from the pan and keep warm in a bowl, discarding any that remain closed.

3 Roughly chop the celery leaves, reserving a few for garnish. Add the chopped leaves, cream and parsley to the cooking juices and season again if necessary. Bring to the boil, then spoon over the mussels. Garnish with celery leaves.

Eat these creamy mussels in true Belgian style. They are good with a plate of thin chips and mayonnaise – as well as a glass of white wine or a fruity Belgian beer.

TIGER PRAWN, MANGETOUT AND MANGO STIR FRY

Serves 4
Preparation 15 mins
Cooking 5 mins

Calories 221
Fat 7g

Simplicity

- 2 x 200g packs raw peeled tiger prawns, defrosted if frozen, rinsed and dried
- 2 tbsp vegetable oil
- 1½ tbsp finely grated fresh root ginger
- 300g pack mangetout
- Bunch of spring onions, sliced
- 1 large ripe mango, peeled and thinly sliced
- 2 tbsp light soy sauce

1 Cut a slit along the back of each prawn with a sharp knife and remove any thin black vein.

2 Heat the oil in a wok, add the ginger and prawns and stir-fry for 2 minutes or until the prawns are just turning pink. Add the mangetout and spring onions and stir-fry for a further minute to soften slightly. Stir in the mango and soy sauce and stir-fry for 1 minute to heat through.

Succulent prawns, crunchy mangetout and juicy mango are flavoured with soy sauce and fresh ginger. Best of all, you can get this dish on the table in 20 minutes. Serve with rice.

SCALLOPS WITH COURGETTES IN APPLE BUTTER

Simplicity 2

Serves 2
Preparation 10 mins
Cooking 5 mins

Calories 327
Fat 18g

- 2 courgettes, cut into 2.5cm (1in) thick slices
- 8 large scallops with their corals
- 1 tbsp olive oil
- Salt and black pepper
- 75ml (3fl oz) apple juice
- 25g (1oz) butter
- Fresh flat-leaf parsley to garnish

1 Turn the courgette slices and scallops gently in the oil and season.

2 Heat a large heavy-based frying pan until hot, add the courgette slices and cook for 2 minutes on one side. Turn over the courgettes and add the scallops to the pan. Cook for 1 minute, then turn over the scallops. Cook both the scallops and courgettes for a further minute, until the scallops are golden and the courgettes are browned.

3 Remove the scallops and courgette slices from the pan and keep warm. Pour the apple juice into the pan, add the butter and cook until reduced to a syrupy sauce. Spoon the sauce over the scallops and courgette slices and garnish with parsley.

Scallops are expensive but delicious, so save this dish for a special treat for two. Make sure you sear them over a high heat; that way they'll be sealed and really tender.

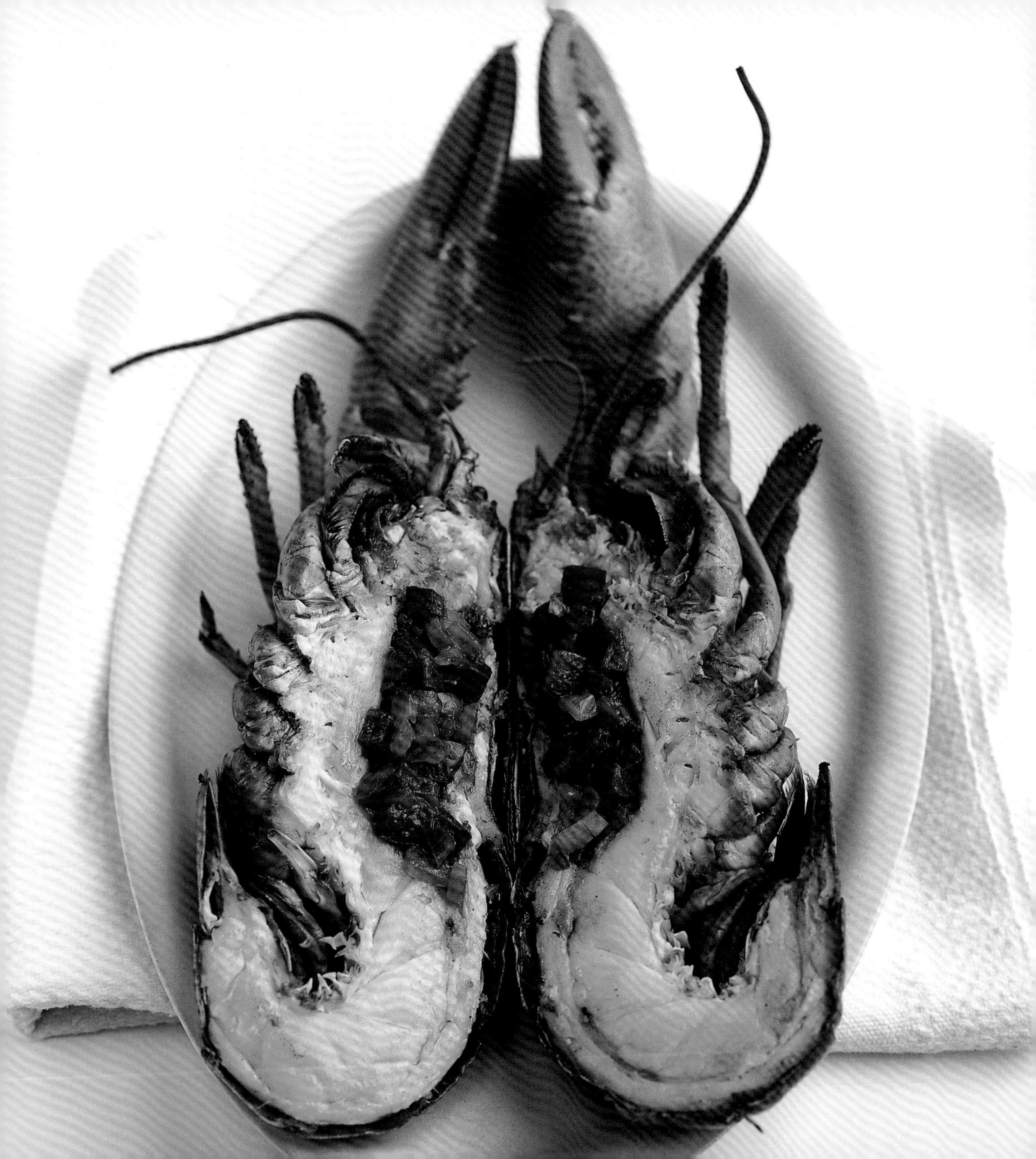

GRILLED LOBSTER WITH CHILLI SALSA

Serves 2
Preparation 20 mins
Cooking 8 mins

Calories 270
Fat 22g

Simplicity 

1 To make the salsa, heat the oil in a saucepan and fry the red pepper, onion and chilli for 5 minutes or until tender. Stir in the tomato purée and season to taste. Transfer to a bowl.

2 To cut the lobsters in half lengthways, turn one on its back. Cut through the head end first, using a large, sharp knife, then turn the lobster round and cut through the tail end. Discard the small greyish 'sac' in the head – everything else in the shell is edible. Crack the large claws with a small hammer or wooden rolling pin. Repeat with the second lobster. Drizzle the cut side of the lobsters with the oil and sprinkle with the cayenne pepper.

3 Heat a large non-stick frying pan or ridged cast iron grill pan until very hot, then add the lobster halves, cut-side down, and cook for 2-3 minutes, until lightly golden. Serve with the salsa.

2 cooked lobsters, about 350g (12oz) each
4 tsp olive oil
Cayenne pepper

For the salsa

2 tbsp olive oil
1 red pepper, deseeded and diced
1 small onion, chopped
1 large red chilli, deseeded and finely chopped
1 tbsp sun-dried tomato purée
Salt and black pepper

If you want to impress somebody, this is the perfect dish! Boiled new potatoes, light spicy salsa and a green salad are great with it. In summer, you can barbecue the lobsters.

INDEX